"Of course I want to live"

Jean-Michel Basquiat

We dedicate this book to those who inspired it

Robin Blake

Kimberly L. Gordon

Jaidyn Henderson

Ernest Odom

Annette Walls

ISBN

978-0-578-80746-1

TIRED

/ˈtī(ə)rd/

In need of sleep or rest; weary; exhausted.

"And I must say tonight that a riot is the language of the unheard. And what is it America has failed to hear? ... It has failed to hear that the promises of freedom and justice have not been met. And it has failed to hear that large segments of white society are more concerned about tranquility and the status quo than about justice and humanity."

— Martin Luther King Jr.

Sick and Tired

Fight or Flight

Seattle ~~police~~ People

Blake

Say His Name

Love + Rage

Blake

Protect Washington's People; Protect Black Lives

Blake

Blake

Everyone isn't Free

White Silence...

Fists Up

Zero Cares

...Ready

What if it was YOUR Son?

St. Julian

Bombs over Baghd....Dallas

St. Julian

Posted...... Toasted

St. Julian

Destruction is Inevitable

One vs Many

Martial Law

St. Julian

SWAT …no safety

Tried and Tired

"Now You See Us"

St. Julian

Free..Doom

Dearest Ken...

St. Julian

F-12

Glass Shatters Easier than Flesh

Necessity?

St. Julian

Cops go Bang

Jesus Take the Wheel

St. Julian

St. Julian

Anonymous

I'm Human

Not Until…

St. Julian

What Ever Happened to Protect and Serve?

St. Julian

No Justice, No Peace

St. Julian

White Silence = Violence

Where's the Justice?

St. Julian

They Do Matter

Untitled

Untitled

St. Julian

Is Kneeling Enough?

Kolor Kan Kill

St. Julian

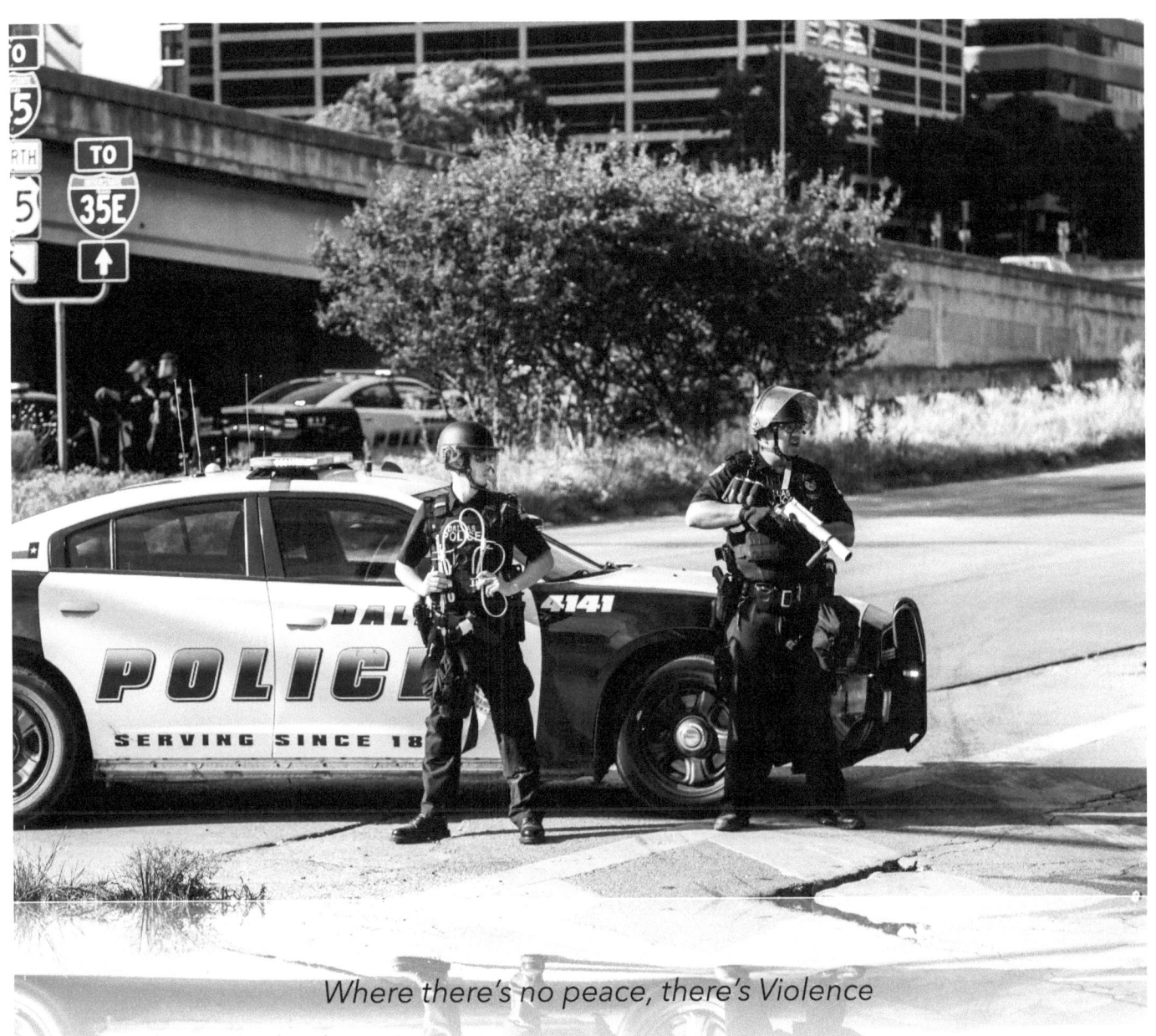

Where there's no peace, there's Violence

St. Julian

Loaded

We Know Who You Are

St. Julian

St. Julian

I'm Proud to be Myself

Odom

CAN'T Breathe

St. Julian

The Vision is Clear

Odom

Ride for our people

Odom

All Too Familiar

Odom

Aaron Bailey | Akai Gurley | Albert Joseph Davis | Alexia Christian | Alonzo Smith | Alteria Woods | Alton Sterling | Anthony Ashford | Anthony Hil | Antronie Scott | Antwon Rose II | Asshams Pharaoh Manley | Atatianna Jefferson | Aura Rosser | Benni Lee Signor | Bettie Jones | Billy Ray Davis | Botham Jean | Brendon Glenn | Breonna Taylor | Brian Keith Day | Calin Roquemore | Christian Taylor | Christopher Davis | Christopher McCorvey | Christopher Whitfield | Dante Parker | Darius Robinson | Darrius Stewart | David Joseph | Demarcus Semer | Dominic Hutchinson | Dominique Clayton | Dyzhawn Perkins | Eric Garner | Eric Harris | Eric Reason | Ezell Ford | Felix Kumi | Frank Smart | Freddie Gray | Gabriella Nevarez | George Floyd | George Mann | India Kager | Jamar Clark | Janet Wilson | Janisha

#SayTheirNames

Fonville | Jerame Reid | John Crawford III | Jonathan Sanders | Jordan Edwards | Joseph Mann | Junior Prosper | Keith Childress Jr. | Keith Harrison McLeod | Kevin Hicks | Kevin Matthews | LaVante Biggs | Lamontez Jones | Laquan McDonald | Marco Loud | Mary Truxillo | Matthew Ajibade | Michael Brown | Michael Lee Marshall | Michael Lorenzo Dean | Michael Noel | Michael Sabbie | Michelle Cusseaux | Miguel Espinal | Mya Hall | Natasha McKenna | Nathaniel Harris Pickett | Pamela Turner | Paterson Brown | Paul O'Neal | Peter Gaines | Philando Castille | Philip White | Quintonio Legrier | Randy Nelson | Richard Perkins | Ronell Foster | Rumain Brisbon | Salvado Ellswood | Samuel Dubose | Sandra Bland | Stephon Clark | Sylville Smith | Tamir Rice | Tanisha Anderson | Terrence Crutcher | Terrill Thomas | Tony Robinson | Torrey Robinson | Troy Robinson | Tyree Crawford | Victor Manuel Larosa | Walter Scott | Wendell Celestine | William Chapman II | Willie Tillman

Seas

Odom

Untitled

Odom

What it does cuz

Scream it

Heart Cry

Cry Out

Odom

End Racism

St. Julian

I am Tamir, I am Trayvon, I am YOU

St. Julian

Systemic Injustice is Deadly

TI'ED

/ˈtī(ə)rd/

Refer to "Tired"

We. Are. Tired.

America's History. Let them tell it; the civil rights movement has an end date.
As we know it; it is 2020 and the civil unrest of our communities continue to dominate.
It's lined with black death and filled with entitlement.
At the hands of America's culprit, and by the calls of America's KKKaren's.

We. Are. Tired.

Exhausted that this has become mundane.
This cycle of: "but I feared for my life", #SayTheirNames, "..but all lives matter!", "but our justice does not look the same!"
"What about Black on Black crime?"
"What about America towards Black LIVES?"

We. Are. Tired.

Now allies rise up all over the nation.
We rock with "Freedom Riders" of this new generation.
White silence equals violence. This revelation is about damn time!
The bigotry resurrected with Trumps tagline. "Make America Great Again". That "again" part did it.
Manifested the evil that lurked in the corners of the slave master's hearts.
Your ancestors! They did this.

We. Are. Tired.

One pandemic surfaced in the midst of another. All boiled over when George Floyd cried out to his dead mother.
Murdered at the hands of those assigned to "protect and serve".
Embezzlement by death bonds and Black bodies.
An American custom the cops preserve.
It isn't enough we already fight for a seat in America's economics.
Where the f**k are these liberties we were promised?

Laupua

Contributing Authors

Akeem Blake
Seattle, WA

Queisha Laupua
Richland, WA

Evan Odom
Houston, TX

Gwen St. Julian
New York, NY | Dallas, TX

Dennis Walls
Houston, TX